My African Caribbean Community

Mosaic designed and made with children at Cabot School 2001 Barbara Disney

Kate Taylor and Luchiano Barnes

Photography by Chris Fairclough

FRANKLIN WATTS
LONDON • SYDNEY

First published in 2005 by
Franklin Watts
96 Leonard Street
London
EC2A 4XD

Franklin Watts Australia
45-51 Huntley Street
Alexandria
NSW 2015

ISBN: 0 7496 5880 0

A CIP catalogue record for this book
is available from the British Library

Printed in Malaysia
Planning and production by Discovery Books Limited
Editor: Laura Durman
Designer: Ian Winton

The author, packager and publisher would like to thank the following people for their
participation in this book:
    Luchi's family
    Luchi's friends
    Corey Johnson
    Garnet Tashiwa-Pinnock
    Kareen Burton
    Full Circle St. Paul's Youth & Family Project
    Vanessa Beckford
    Colston's Primary School
    Head Teacher Mr Gavaghan
    Mr Scott
    Beverley Forbes & Plantation
    Zetland Evangelical Church and Sunday School
    Grosvenor Supermarket
    Jonny at Jon's Fruit & Veg & Afro-Caribbean food

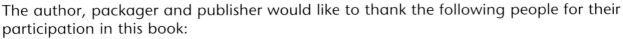

Contents

All About Me   4

My Family   6

Where I Live   8

Jamaica   10

Shops   12

School   14

My Friends   16

Food   18

My Hobbies   20

Languages   22

Clothes   24

Religion   26

Carnival!   28

I Like Bristol   30

Glossary   31

Index   32

All About Me

My name is Luchiano Barnes but my friends call me Luchi. I'm 8 years old.

My family originally came from Jamaica. I live in St Paul's in Bristol with my mum, my two sisters and my grandmother. I call my grandmother nanny.

◀ This is a street in St Paul's.

I share a room with my 3-year-old sister, Ria. We've got a bunk bed and I sleep on the top. I like sharing a room with her. Anya, my little sister, is 7 months old and sleeps in my mum's bedroom.

▶ **Me with Ria (right) and Anya outside our house.**

My Family

Most of my family live in Bristol and I see them all the time. I always have someone to play with.

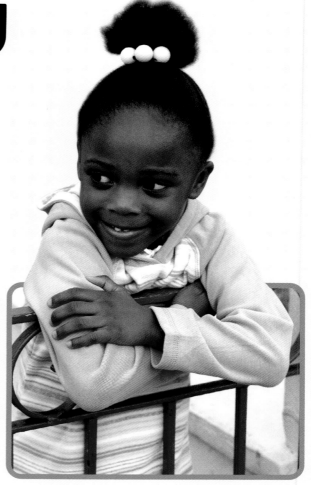

▲ **My sister, Ria.**

My mum, Rachel, and my dad, Patrick, were both born in Bristol. We lived in Jamaica for a while but moved back when I was 4 years old.

◀ **My mum with Anya.**

My nanny, Joan, came over from Jamaica on her own 40 years ago to work as a nurse in a hospital.

◀ **This is a picture of my nanny (left) when she came to England.**

Some of my aunts, uncles and cousins live nearby. I play with my 9-year-old cousin Aleyah a lot.

▶ **Me with Aleyah.**

Where I Live

I like living in St Paul's. It's noisy and busy and people look out for each other.

You can always hear music coming from the other houses in my street because my neighbours play *reggae* and *rap* really loud. It's nice to listen to, unless I'm trying to get to sleep!

▶ **This is the street where I live.**

I play in a park near my house called New Park. It's got a climbing frame and a curly slide that Ria likes. I play basketball and football there with my friends.

▶ **Me in the park with my friends.**

◀ **Me playing basketball in the park.**

St Paul's can be a bit rough. Gangs hang around at the end of my road and sometimes they have fights. But they don't bother me and I like living here.

9

Jamaica

I had a good time when we lived in Jamaica. The beaches were great, and it was always warm! Here are some pictures of me then. I was much younger.

In Jamaica, my mum and dad had a really big house in a place called Village Green.

▲ Me in Village Green.

◀ Me watering the flowers outside my house.

There was a swimming pool nearby that I swam in every day.

▶ **Me in the swimming pool.**

My dad used to take me to the riverbank to catch *lobsters*. I carried them home and we'd eat them for dinner. It was good fun!

Sometimes we stayed with my great granny, my nanny's mum. She was really nice and had lots of cats in her house.

◀ **Me with nanny at my great granny's house.**

Shops

I spend my pocket money in the local shops. I can buy all sorts of things.

There are a few little shops near where I live that I'm allowed to walk to on my own. Ria and I buy lollies from the newsagents in the summer.

Sometimes mum takes us into Bristol city centre. There are lots of shops, but at the weekends it's really busy.

◀ Me with Ria in Bristol city centre.

My nanny goes to a special shop to buy Jamaican vegetables. Sometimes I go with her. There's loads to choose from.

▼ **Me and nanny at the vegetable shop.**

◀ **People grow bananas in Jamaica. They're my favourite fruit.**

▼ **This is a *cassava*. My mum grates it, washes it and then fries it in little, round cakes called '*bammies*'. Yum!**

▲ **This is a *sweet potato*. It's bright orange inside!**

13

School

My school is called Colston's Primary School, and my teacher, Mr Scott, is brilliant.

► Mr Scott helping me with my work.

My favourite lesson is PE. I'm a really good runner. Sometimes I run all the way to school, which is up a big hill called Nine Tree Hill. Everyone walks and huffs up it, but I run!

◄ My PE lesson.

I like history lessons too. It's really interesting finding out about things that have happened in the past.

▶ **Me looking for information for my history project.**

At break time I usually play a game called 'Releasers' with my friends. You have to run off and hide and then try to get back to base without being caught. It's really fun and because I like running, I'm quite good at it.

◀ **Me with my friends at break time.**

My Friends

I've got lots of friends at school, but my best friends are Corey, Garnet and Kareen.

▶ **Me with my school friends.**

Corey is my cousin. He lives in America but comes to stay with us every summer.

We do loads of things together. It's great having him living with us.

◀ **Me with Corey.**

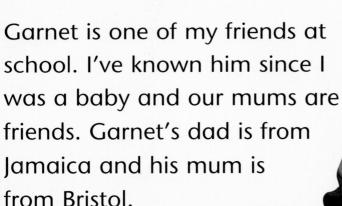

▼ **Me playing football with Garnet (middle) and Kareen (left).**

Garnet is one of my friends at school. I've known him since I was a baby and our mums are friends. Garnet's dad is from Jamaica and his mum is from Bristol.

▶ **Garnet.**

My friend Kareen goes to my school too. He lives nearby so I often see him at weekends.

Food

I love it when we have mashed potatoes, baked beans, sausages and salad for dinner. They're the best!

My mum and nanny like to have their dinner quite late, so I usually eat just with Ria.

I like fruit and vegetables, especially a Jamaican vegetable called *chocho*. It looks like an apple and tastes a bit like a courgette. We have it in soup.

▶ This is a chocho.

We went to a restaurant called Plantation, for my mum's birthday. She had *jerk pork* and I had *jerk chicken*. It's a spicy Jamaican dish. I think it's really great!

◀ **Me eating jerk chicken.**

▼ **My family eating at Plantation.**

My Hobbies

I usually spend my spare time with my friends, and I have lots of hobbies.

I like riding my bike. My mum allows me to go as far as her friend's house. She knows our neighbours will look out of their windows to make sure I'm OK.

▼ **Me with Corey playing on my Game Boy.**

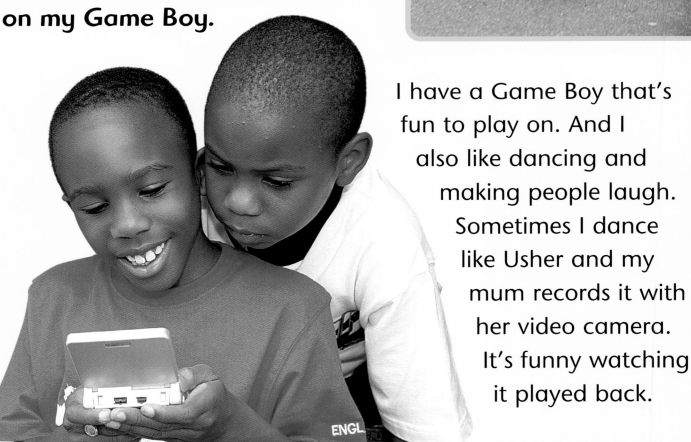

I have a Game Boy that's fun to play on. And I also like dancing and making people laugh. Sometimes I dance like Usher and my mum records it with her video camera. It's funny watching it played back.

I like playing basketball and football too.

▶ **Me practising my football skills in the park.**

◀ **I play cards with Ria a lot.**

Languages

I speak English all of the time, but speak a different type of English, called *Patois*, with my dad.

English is the only language my family speak, and people in Jamaica use it too. But sometimes Jamaicans speak Patois, which is like slang. My dad talks to me in Patois all the time and I can understand some of it. He can't always understand me when I speak to him in English, though.

▲ Me talking to my mum.

◀ Me talking to my dad on the phone.

I am starting to learn French at school, which I enjoy. I think it's really good to learn other languages because then you can talk to people when you're in their country.

▼ **Me doing my French homework.**

Clothes

I wear jeans most of the time, with a t-shirt and trainers.

Sometimes I dress like my favourite rapper, 50 Cent. He wears jewellery a lot. I've got some big chains and rings, and two beaded necklaces that my mum bought me. I like wearing jewellery, but I'm not allowed to wear it to school.

▶ **Me dressed like 50 Cent.**

Ria doesn't wear jewellery, but she has lots of different hair bobbles. My mum sometimes *braids* her hair. I think that looks good. When it's not braided though, it's really curly, which is nice too.

▶ **My mum doing Ria's hair.**

There is a uniform at my school but you only have to wear it if you want to, so sometimes I do and sometimes I don't.

◀ **Me in my school uniform.**

25

Religion

My family are Christians and I go to church every Sunday with Ria.

A bus comes to our house to pick us up. Our church has a Sunday school where I learn all about my religion. We also sing songs and read stories from the Bible. I really like going there.

▶ **Me talking to the vicar at our church.**

26

Ria and I pray in church, and also every night before we go to sleep. I like praying, it makes me feel like a good person.

▶ **Me and Ria at Sunday school.**

On Saturdays, I go to a kids' club in St Paul's called Full Circle. We learn about other faiths and look at their holy books. I think it's good to know about other religions.

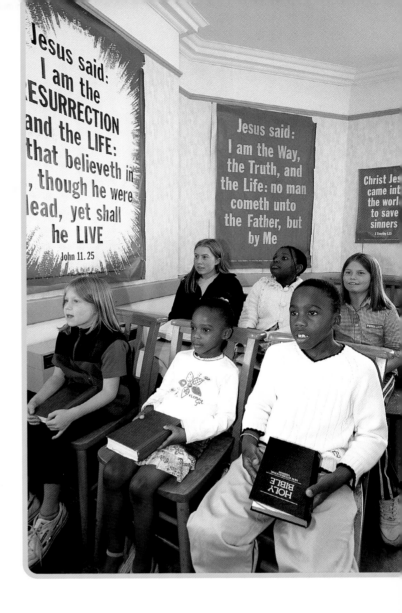

◀ **Me praying at Sunday school.**

Carnival!

My community has a big celebration each year called Carnival.

The St Paul's Carnival is a street festival with colourful floats, dancing and singing.

It's really fun and it's a time when my community joins together to welcome people from all over Bristol, and Britain. We met a family last year who had travelled all the way from Manchester.

▲ People wear amazing costumes.

◀ Ria walked in the Carnival procession this year with her school.

◀ These children are in my kids' club, Full Circle.

We eat traditional Jamaican food like curried goat, rice with peas, and sugar cane. My nanny usually has a food stall outside our house. She's a brilliant cook! Carnival is always on the first Saturday in July. People celebrate it in Jamaica as well.

▼ A man cooking jerk chicken on the barbecue.

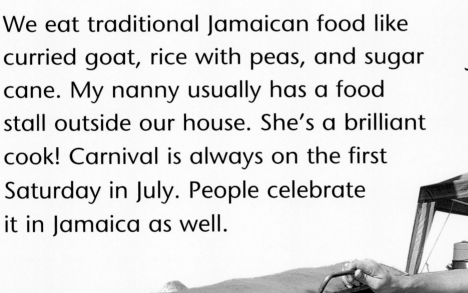

I Like Bristol

I love living in Bristol. One day I'd like to live in a bigger house and, when I become a famous runner, maybe I will. I think I will still want to live in Bristol though.

Glossary

Bammies Small, round cakes made from grated cassava. They are fried in oil, and often eaten with butter and fried fish.

Braids These are small, tight plaits.

Cassava This vegetable is very popular in warm countries where it is grown. People have to cook it in a certain way though, because it can be poisonous.

Chocho A vegetable that comes from a plant called a chayote.

Jerk pork or chicken A spicy Jamaican dish. Traditionally, the meat is covered in spices and cooked over a wood fire.

Lobster An animal that lives in the sea. It has a shell, a long body, eight legs and two large claws.

Patois A type of English which is a bit like slang.

Rap A type of music from America, in which people speak really fast in time with the beat.

Reggae A style of music from Jamaica.

Sweet potato A vegetable that grows in warm countries, like Jamaica.